MW00963785

Address Book

This belongs to

BARBOUR
PUBLISHING, INC.
Uhrichsville, Ohio

a

Name

Address

Phone ( ) E-mail

Name

Address

Phone ( ) E-mail

Name

Address

Phone ( ) E-mail

Name

Address

Phone ( ) E-mail

Name

Address

Phone ( ) E-mail

a

Name

Address

Phone (   )   E-mail

Name

Address

Phone (   )   E-mail

Name

Address

Phone (   )   E-mail

Name

Address

Phone (   )   E-mail

Name

Address

Phone (   )   E-mail

a

Name

Address

Phone ( ) E-mail

Name

Address

Phone ( ) E-mail

Name

Address

Phone ( ) E-mail

Name

Address

Phone ( ) E-mail

Name

Address

Phone ( ) E-mail

ame _____

dress _____

one (____) _____ E-mail _____

ame _____

dress _____

one (____) _____ E-mail _____

ame _____

dress _____

one (____) _____ E-mail _____

ame _____

dress _____

one (____) _____ E-mail _____

ame _____

dress _____

one (____) _____ E-mail _____

b

Name _____

Address _____

_____

Phone ( ) _____ E-mail _____

Name _____

Address _____

_____

Phone ( ) _____ E-mail _____

Name _____

Address _____

_____

Phone ( ) _____ E-mail _____

Name _____

Address _____

_____

Phone ( ) _____ E-mail _____

Name _____

Address _____

_____

Phone ( ) _____ E-mail _____

_b_

ame _____

ddress _____

_____

hone ( ) _____ E-mail _____

ame _____

ddress _____

_____

hone ( ) _____ E-mail _____

ame _____

ddress _____

_____

hone ( ) _____ E-mail _____

ame _____

ddress _____

_____

hone ( ) _____ E-mail _____

ame _____

ddress _____

_____

hone ( ) _____ E-mail _____

b

Name

Address

Phone ( ) E-mail

Name

Address

Phone ( ) E-mail

Name

Address

Phone ( ) E-mail

Name

Address

Phone ( ) E-mail

Name

Address

Phone ( ) E-mail

_b_

Name

Address

Phone (   )   E-mail

Name

Address

Phone (   )   E-mail

Name

Address

Phone (   )   E-mail

Name

Address

Phone (   )   E-mail

Name

Address

Phone (   )   E-mail

C

Name _____

Address _____

_____

Phone (___) _____ E-mail _____

Name _____

Address _____

_____

Phone (___) _____ E-mail _____

Name _____

Address _____

_____

Phone (___) _____ E-mail _____

Name _____

Address _____

_____

Phone (___) _____ E-mail _____

Name _____

Address _____

_____

Phone (___) _____ E-mail _____

C

Name _____

Address _____

Phone (___) _____ E-mail _____

Name _____

Address _____

Phone (___) _____ E-mail _____

Name _____

Address _____

Phone (___) _____ E-mail _____

Name _____

Address _____

Phone (___) _____ E-mail _____

Name _____

Address _____

Phone (___) _____ E-mail _____

C

Name _____

Address _____

_____

Phone (____) _____ E-mail _____

Name _____

Address _____

_____

Phone (____) _____ E-mail _____

Name _____

Address _____

_____

Phone (____) _____ E-mail _____

Name _____

Address _____

_____

Phone (____) _____ E-mail _____

Name _____

Address _____

_____

Phone (____) _____ E-mail _____

Name _____

Address _____

_____

C

Phone ( ) _____ E-mail _____

Name _____

Address _____

_____

Phone ( ) _____ E-mail _____

Name _____

Address _____

_____

Phone ( ) _____ E-mail _____

Name _____

Address _____

_____

Phone ( ) _____ E-mail _____

Name _____

Address _____

_____

Phone ( ) _____ E-mail _____

d

Name

Address

Phone ( ) E-mail

Name

Address

Phone ( ) E-mail

Name

Address

Phone ( ) E-mail

Name

Address

Phone ( ) E-mail

Name

Address

Phone ( ) E-mail

Name

Address

Phone ( ) E-mail

d

Name

Address

Phone ( ) E-mail

Name

Address

Phone ( ) E-mail

Name

Address

Phone ( ) E-mail

Name

Address

Phone ( ) E-mail

d

Name

Address

Phone ( )   E-mail

Name

Address

Phone ( )   E-mail

Name

Address

Phone ( )   E-mail

Name

Address

Phone ( )   E-mail

Name

Address

Phone ( )   E-mail

Name _____

Address _____

_____

Phone ( ) _____ E-mail _____

Name _____

Address _____

_____

Phone ( ) _____ E-mail _____

Name _____

Address _____

_____

Phone ( ) _____ E-mail _____

Name _____

Address _____

_____

Phone ( ) _____ E-mail _____

Name _____

Address _____

_____

Phone ( ) _____ E-mail _____

d

e

Name _____

Address _____

_____

Phone (___) _____ E-mail _____

Name _____

Address _____

_____

Phone (___) _____ E-mail _____

Name _____

Address _____

_____

Phone (___) _____ E-mail _____

Name _____

Address _____

_____

Phone (___) _____ E-mail _____

Name _____

Address _____

_____

Phone (___) _____ E-mail _____

Name

Address

Phone ( ) E-mail

e

Name

Address

Phone ( ) E-mail

Name

Address

Phone ( ) E-mail

Name

Address

Phone ( ) E-mail

Name

Address

Phone ( ) E-mail

e

Name

Address

Phone ( )   E-mail

Name

Address

Phone ( )   E-mail

Name

Address

Phone ( )   E-mail

Name

Address

Phone ( )   E-mail

Name

Address

Phone ( )   E-mail

Name

Address

Phone ( )   E-mail

e

Name

Address

Phone ( )   E-mail

Name

Address

Phone ( )   E-mail

Name

Address

Phone ( )   E-mail

Name

Address

Phone ( )   E-mail

f

Name

Address

Phone ( ) E-mail

Name

Address

Phone ( ) E-mail

Name

Address

Phone ( ) E-mail

Name

Address

Phone ( ) E-mail

Name

Address

Phone ( ) E-mail

ame _____

ddress _____

hone ( ) _____ E-mail _____

ame _____

ddress _____

_f_

hone ( ) _____ E-mail _____

ame _____

ddress _____

hone ( ) _____ E-mail _____

ame _____

ddress _____

hone ( ) _____ E-mail _____

ame _____

ddress _____

hone ( ) _____ E-mail _____

f

Name

Address

Phone ( )   E-mail

Name

Address

Phone ( )   E-mail

Name

Address

Phone ( )   E-mail

Name

Address

Phone ( )   E-mail

Name

Address

Phone ( )   E-mail

Name _____

Address _____

Phone (___) _____ E-mail _____

Name _____

Address _____

f

Phone (___) _____ E-mail _____

Name _____

Address _____

Phone (___) _____ E-mail _____

Name _____

Address _____

Phone (___) _____ E-mail _____

Name _____

Address _____

Phone (___) _____ E-mail _____

g

Name

Address

Phone ( ) E-mail

Name

Address

Phone ( ) E-mail

Name

Address

Phone ( ) E-mail

Name

Address

Phone ( ) E-mail

Name

Address

Phone ( ) E-mail

Name _____

Address _____

_____

Phone ( ) _____ E-mail _____

Name _____

Address _____

_____

Phone ( ) _____ E-mail _____

Name _____

Address _____

_____

Phone ( ) _____ E-mail _____

Name _____

Address _____

_____

Phone ( ) _____ E-mail _____

Name _____

Address _____

_____

Phone ( ) _____ E-mail _____

g

Name _____

Address _____

_____

Phone (_____) _____ E-mail _____

Name _____

Address _____

_____

Phone (_____) _____ E-mail _____

Name _____

Address _____

_____

Phone (_____) _____ E-mail _____

Name _____

Address _____

_____

Phone (_____) _____ E-mail _____

Name _____

Address _____

_____

Phone (_____) _____ E-mail _____

ame

ddress

none ( )   E-mail

ame

ddress

none ( )   E-mail

g

ame

ddress

ione ( )   E-mail

ame

ddress

ione ( )   E-mail

ame

ddress

ione ( )   E-mail

h

Name

Address

Phone (   )   E-mail

Name

Address

Phone (   )   E-mail

Name

Address

Phone (   )   E-mail

Name

Address

Phone (   )   E-mail

Name

Address

Phone (   )   E-mail

ame _____

dress _____

_____

one (___) _____ E-mail _____

ame _____

dress _____

_____

one (___) _____ E-mail _____

h

me _____

dress _____

_____

one (___) _____ E-mail _____

me _____

dress _____

_____

one (___) _____ E-mail _____

me _____

dress _____

_____

one (___) _____ E-mail _____

h

Name

Address

Phone ( ) E-mail

Name

Address

Phone ( ) E-mail

Name

Address

Phone ( ) E-mail

Name

Address

Phone ( ) E-mail

Name

Address

Phone ( ) E-mail

ne

ress

ne ( ) E-mail

ne

ress

ne ( ) E-mail

ne

ress

ne ( ) E-mail

ne

ress

ne ( ) E-mail

ne

ress

ne ( ) E-mail

h

Name

Address

Phone (   ) E-mail

Name

Address

Phone (   ) E-mail

Name

Address

Phone (   ) E-mail

Name

Address

Phone (   ) E-mail

Name

Address

Phone (   ) E-mail

me _____

dress _____

one ( ) _____ E-mail _____

me _____

dress _____

one ( ) _____ E-mail _____

me _____

dress _____

one ( ) _____ E-mail _____

me _____

dress _____

one ( ) _____ E-mail _____

me _____

dress _____

one ( ) _____ E-mail _____

Name

Address

Phone (   )   E-mail

Name

Address

Phone (   )   E-mail

Name

Address

Phone (   )   E-mail

Name

Address

Phone (   )   E-mail

Name

Address

Phone (   )   E-mail

me _____

dress _____

one (___) _____   E-mail _____

me _____

dress _____

one (___) _____   E-mail _____

me _____

dress _____

one (___) _____   E-mail _____

ne _____

dress _____

ne (___) _____   E-mail _____

ne _____

ress _____

ne (___) _____   E-mail _____

Name

Address

Phone (   )   E-mail

Name

Address

Phone (   )   E-mail

j

Name

Address

Phone (   )   E-mail

Name

Address

Phone (   )   E-mail

Name

Address

Phone (   )   E-mail

me _____

dress _____

one ( ) _____ E-mail _____

me _____

dress _____

one ( ) _____ E-mail _____

me _____

dress _____

_j_

ne ( ) _____ E-mail _____

me _____

ress _____

ne ( ) _____ E-mail _____

me _____

ress _____

ne ( ) _____ E-mail _____

j

Name

Address

Phone ( )   E-mail

Name

Address

Phone ( )   E-mail

Name

Address

Phone ( )   E-mail

Name

Address

Phone ( )   E-mail

Name

Address

Phone ( )   E-mail

me _____

dress _____

one (___) _____ E-mail _____

me _____

dress _____

one (___) _____ E-mail _____

me _____

dress _____

j

one (___) _____ E-mail _____

me _____

dress _____

one (___) _____ E-mail _____

me _____

dress _____

one (___) _____ E-mail _____

Name _____

Address _____

_____

Phone ( ) _____ E-mail _____

Name _____

Address _____

_____

Phone ( ) _____ E-mail _____

Name _____

Address _____

_____

k

Phone ( ) _____ E-mail _____

Name _____

Address _____

_____

Phone ( ) _____ E-mail _____

Name _____

Address _____

_____

Phone ( ) _____ E-mail _____

Name

Address

Phone ( )   E-mail

Name

Address

Phone ( )   E-mail

Name

Address

Phone ( )   E-mail

Name

Address

Phone ( )   E-mail

Name

Address

Phone ( )   E-mail

k

Name _____

Address _____

_____

Phone (____) _____ E-mail _____

Name _____

Address _____

_____

Phone (____) _____ E-mail _____

Name _____

Address _____

_____

_k_

Phone (____) _____ E-mail _____

Name _____

Address _____

_____

Phone (____) _____ E-mail _____

Name _____

Address _____

_____

Phone (____) _____ E-mail _____

Name

Address

Phone ( ) E-mail

Name

Address

Phone ( ) E-mail

Name

Address

Phone ( ) E-mail

Name

Address

Phone ( ) E-mail

Name

Address

Phone ( ) E-mail

Name

Address

Phone ( ) E-mail

k

Name _____

Address _____

_____

Phone (____) _____ E-mail _____

Name _____

Address _____

_____

Phone (____) _____ E-mail _____

Name _____

Address _____

_____

Phone (____) _____ E-mail _____

l

Name _____

Address _____

_____

Phone (____) _____ E-mail _____

Name _____

Address _____

_____

Phone (____) _____ E-mail _____

ame

ddress

none ( ) E-mail

ame

ddress

none ( ) E-mail

ame

ddress

one ( ) E-mail

ame

dress

one ( ) E-mail

ame

dress

one ( ) E-mail

Name

Address

Phone ( )   E-mail

Name

Address

Phone ( )   E-mail

Name

Address

Phone ( )   E-mail

l

Name

Address

Phone ( )   E-mail

Name

Address

Phone ( )   E-mail

Name _____

Address _____

Phone ( ) _____ E-mail _____

Name _____

Address _____

Phone ( ) _____ E-mail _____

Name _____

Address _____

Phone ( ) _____ E-mail _____

Name _____

Address _____

Phone ( ) _____ E-mail _____

Name _____

Address _____

Phone ( ) _____ E-mail _____

Name

Address

Phone (　　　) 　　　　　　　　E-mail

Name

Address

Phone (　　　) 　　　　　　　　E-mail

Name

Address

Phone (　　　) 　　　　　　　　E-mail

Name

M

Address

Phone (　　　) 　　　　　　　　E-mail

Name

Address

Phone (　　　) 　　　　　　　　E-mail

Name _____

Address _____

Phone ( ) _____ E-mail _____

Name _____

Address _____

Phone ( ) _____ E-mail _____

Name _____

Address _____

Phone ( ) _____ E-mail _____

Name _____

Address _____

M

Phone ( ) _____ E-mail _____

Name _____

Address _____

Phone ( ) _____ E-mail _____

Name

Address

Phone ( ) E-mail

Name

Address

Phone ( ) E-mail

Name

Address

Phone ( ) E-mail

Name

Address

Phone ( ) E-mail

Name

Address

Phone ( ) E-mail

m

Name

Address

Phone ( )   E-mail

Name

Address

Phone ( )   E-mail

Name

Address

Phone ( )   E-mail

Name

Address

Phone ( )   E-mail

Name

Address

Phone ( )   E-mail

M

Name

Address

Phone ( )   E-mail

Name

Address

Phone ( )   E-mail

Name

Address

Phone ( )   E-mail

Name

Address

n

Phone ( )   E-mail

Name

Address

Phone ( )   E-mail

Name

Address

Phone ( )   E-mail

Name

Address

Phone ( )   E-mail

Name

Address

Phone ( )   E-mail

Name

Address

Phone ( )   E-mail

Name

Address

Phone ( )   E-mail

n

Name

Address

Phone (   )   E-mail

Name

Address

Phone (   )   E-mail

Name

Address

Phone (   )   E-mail

Name

Address

Phone (   )   E-mail

n

Name

Address

Phone (   )   E-mail

Name

Address

Phone (   ) E-mail

Name

Address

Phone (   ) E-mail

Name

Address

Phone (   ) E-mail

Name

Address

Phone (   ) E-mail

Name

Address

Phone (   ) E-mail

N

Name

Address

Phone ( )   E-mail

Name

Address

Phone ( )   E-mail

Name

Address

Phone ( )   E-mail

Name

Address

Phone ( )   E-mail

Name

Address

Phone ( )   E-mail

Name _____

Address _____

_____

Phone ( ) _____ E-mail _____

Name _____

Address _____

_____

Phone ( ) _____ E-mail _____

Name _____

Address _____

_____

Phone ( ) _____ E-mail _____

Name _____

Address _____

_____

Phone ( ) _____ E-mail _____

Name _____

Address _____

_____

Phone ( ) _____ E-mail _____

0

Name

Address

Phone ( )   E-mail

Name

Address

Phone ( )   E-mail

Name

Address

Phone ( )   E-mail

Name

Address

Phone ( )   E-mail

Name

Address

Phone ( )   E-mail

O

ame _____

ddress _____

hone ( ) _____ E-mail _____

ame _____

ddress _____

one ( ) _____ E-mail _____

ame _____

dress _____

one ( ) _____ E-mail _____

ame _____

dress _____

one ( ) _____ E-mail _____

me _____

dress _____

one ( ) _____ E-mail _____

Name

Address

Phone ( )   E-mail

Name

Address

Phone ( )   E-mail

Name

Address

Phone ( )   E-mail

Name

Address

Phone ( )   E-mail

Name

Address

Phone ( )   E-mail

Name

Address

Phone (   ) _____ E-mail _____

Name

Address

Phone (   ) _____ E-mail _____

Name

Address

Phone (   ) _____ E-mail _____

Name

Address

Phone (   ) _____ E-mail _____

Name

Address

Phone (   ) _____ E-mail _____

Name _____

Address _____

_____

Phone ( ) _____ E-mail _____

Name _____

Address _____

_____

Phone ( ) _____ E-mail _____

Name _____

Address _____

_____

Phone ( ) _____ E-mail _____

Name _____

Address _____

_____

Phone ( ) _____ E-mail _____

Name _____

Address _____

_____

Phone ( ) _____ E-mail _____

me _____

dress _____

one ( ) _____ E-mail _____

me _____

dress _____

one ( ) _____ E-mail _____

me _____

dress _____

one ( ) _____ E-mail _____

ne _____

dress _____

ne ( ) _____ E-mail _____

ne _____

ress _____

ne ( ) _____ E-mail _____

Name _____

Address _____

Phone ( ) _____ E-mail _____

Name _____

Address _____

Phone ( ) _____ E-mail _____

Name _____

Address _____

Phone ( ) _____ E-mail _____

Name _____

Address _____

Phone ( ) _____ E-mail _____

Name _____

Address _____

Phone ( ) _____ E-mail _____

ame _____

dress _____

_____

one (___) _____ E-mail _____

ame _____

dress _____

_____

one (___) _____ E-mail _____

me _____

dress _____

_____

one (___) _____ E-mail _____

me _____

dress _____

_____

one (___) _____ E-mail _____

me _____

dress _____

_____

one (___) _____ E-mail _____

R

Name _____

Address _____

_____

Phone (___) _____ E-mail _____

Name _____

Address _____

_____

Phone (___) _____ E-mail _____

Name _____

Address _____

_____

Phone (___) _____ E-mail _____

Name _____

Address _____

_____

Phone (___) _____ E-mail _____

Name _____

Address _____

_____

Phone (___) _____ E-mail _____

me _____

dress _____

one ( ) _____ E-mail _____

me _____

dress _____

one ( ) _____ E-mail _____

me _____

dress _____

one ( ) _____ E-mail _____

me _____

dress _____

one ( ) _____ E-mail _____

me _____

dress _____

one ( ) _____ E-mail _____

Name _____

Address _____

_____

Phone (___) _____ E-mail _____

Name _____

Address _____

_____

Phone (___) _____ E-mail _____

Name _____

Address _____

_____

Phone (___) _____ E-mail _____

Name _____

Address _____

_____

Phone (___) _____ E-mail _____

Name _____

Address _____

_____

Phone (___) _____ E-mail _____

ame _____

ddress _____

_____

none ( ) _____   E-mail _____

ame _____

ddress _____

_____

none ( ) _____   E-mail _____

ame _____

ddress _____

_____

one ( ) _____   E-mail _____

ame _____

ddress _____

_____

one ( ) _____   E-mail _____

ame _____

ddress _____

_____

one ( ) _____   E-mail _____

r

Name _____

Address _____

_____

Phone (_____) _____ E-mail _____

Name _____

Address _____

_____

Phone (_____) _____ E-mail _____

Name _____

Address _____

_____

Phone (_____) _____ E-mail _____

Name _____

Address _____

_____

Phone (_____) _____ E-mail _____

Name _____

Address _____

_____

r

Phone (_____) _____ E-mail _____

ame _____

ddress _____

hone ( ) _____ E-mail _____

ame _____

ddress _____

hone ( ) _____ E-mail _____

ame _____

ddress _____

one ( ) _____ E-mail _____

ame _____

dress _____

one ( ) _____ E-mail _____

ame _____

dress _____

one ( ) _____ E-mail _____

r

Name

Address

Phone ( ) E-mail

Name

Address

Phone ( ) E-mail

Name

Address

Phone ( ) E-mail

Name

Address

Phone ( ) E-mail

Name

Address

Phone ( ) E-mail

Name _____

Address _____

Phone (____) _____ E-mail _____

Name _____

Address _____

Phone (____) _____ E-mail _____

Name _____

Address _____

Phone (____) _____ E-mail _____

Name _____

Address _____

Phone (____) _____ E-mail _____

Name _____

Address _____

Phone (____) _____ E-mail _____

Name

Address

Phone ( ) E-mail

Name

Address

Phone ( ) E-mail

Name

Address

Phone ( ) E-mail

Name

Address

Phone ( ) E-mail

Name

Address

Phone ( ) E-mail

Name _____

Address _____

_____

Phone ( ) _____ E-mail _____

Name _____

Address _____

_____

Phone ( ) _____ E-mail _____

Name _____

Address _____

_____

Phone ( ) _____ E-mail _____

Name _____

Address _____

_____

Phone ( ) _____ E-mail _____

Name _____

Address _____

_____

Phone ( ) _____ E-mail _____

Name

Address

Phone ( ) E-mail

Name

Address

Phone ( ) E-mail

Name

Address

Phone ( ) E-mail

Name

Address

Phone ( ) E-mail

Name

Address

Phone ( ) E-mail

t

Name _____

Address _____

Phone (___) _____ E-mail _____

Name _____

Address _____

Phone (___) _____ E-mail _____

Name _____

Address _____

Phone (___) _____ E-mail _____

Name _____

Address _____

Phone (___) _____ E-mail _____

Name _____

Address _____

t

Phone (___) _____ E-mail _____

Name _____

Address _____

_____

Phone (___) _____ E-mail _____

Name _____

Address _____

_____

Phone (___) _____ E-mail _____

Name _____

Address _____

_____

Phone (___) _____ E-mail _____

Name _____

Address _____

_____

Phone (___) _____ E-mail _____

t

Name _____

Address _____

_____

Phone (___) _____ E-mail _____

Name _____

Address _____

Phone (_____) _____ E-mail _____

Name _____

Address _____

Phone (_____) _____ E-mail _____

Name _____

Address _____

Phone (_____) _____ E-mail _____

Name _____

Address _____

Phone (_____) _____ E-mail _____

Name _____

Address _____

Phone (_____) _____ E-mail _____

Name _____

Address _____

Phone (_____) _____ E-mail _____

t

Name _____

Address _____

_____

Phone (_____) _____ E-mail _____

Name _____

Address _____

_____

Phone (_____) _____ E-mail _____

Name _____

Address _____

_____

Phone (_____) _____ E-mail _____

Name _____

Address _____

_____

Phone (_____) _____ E-mail _____

Name _____

Address _____

_____

Phone (_____) _____ E-mail _____

U

Name _____

Address _____

_____

Phone ( ) _____ E-mail _____

Name _____

Address _____

_____

Phone ( ) _____ E-mail _____

Name _____

Address _____

_____

Phone ( ) _____ E-mail _____

Name _____

Address _____

_____

Phone ( ) _____ E-mail _____

Name _____

Address _____

_____

Phone ( ) _____ E-mail _____

U

Name _____

Address _____

_____

Phone (___) _____ E-mail _____

Name _____

Address _____

_____

Phone (___) _____ E-mail _____

Name _____

Address _____

_____

Phone (___) _____ E-mail _____

Name _____

Address _____

_____

Phone (___) _____ E-mail _____

Name _____

Address _____

_____

Phone (___) _____ E-mail _____

Name _____

Address _____

Phone ( ) _____ E-mail _____

Name _____

Address _____

Phone ( ) _____ E-mail _____

Name _____

Address _____

Phone ( ) _____ E-mail _____

Name _____

Address _____

Phone ( ) _____ E-mail _____

Name _____

Address _____

Phone ( ) _____ E-mail _____

Y

Name _____

Address _____

_____

Phone (___) _____ E-mail _____

Name _____

Address _____

_____

Phone (___) _____ E-mail _____

Name _____

Address _____

_____

Phone (___) _____ E-mail _____

Name _____

Address _____

_____

Phone (___) _____ E-mail _____

Name _____

Address _____

_____

Phone (___) _____ E-mail _____

W

Name

Address

Phone ( )   E-mail

Name

Address

Phone ( )   E-mail

Name

Address

Phone ( )   E-mail

Name

Address

Phone ( )   E-mail

Name

Address

Phone ( )   E-mail

W

Name

Address

Phone ( ) E-mail

Name

Address

Phone ( ) E-mail

Name

Address

Phone ( ) E-mail

Name

W

Address

Phone ( ) E-mail

Name

Address

Phone ( ) E-mail

ame _____

ddress _____

_____

hone ( ) _____ E-mail _____

ame _____

ddress _____

_____

one ( ) _____ E-mail _____

ame _____

ddress _____

_____

one ( ) _____ E-mail _____

ame _____

ddress _____

_____

one ( ) _____ E-mail _____

me _____

dress _____

_____

one ( ) _____ E-mail _____

W

Name _____

Address _____

_____

Phone ( ) _____ E-mail _____

Name _____

Address _____

_____

Phone ( ) _____ E-mail _____

Name _____

Address _____

_____

Phone ( ) _____ E-mail _____

x

Name _____

Address _____

_____

Phone ( ) _____ E-mail _____

Name _____

Address _____

_____

Phone ( ) _____ E-mail _____

ame _____

ddress _____

_____

one ( ) _____ E-mail _____

ame _____

ddress _____

_____

one ( ) _____ E-mail _____

ame _____

dress _____

_____

one ( ) _____ E-mail _____

me _____

dress _____

_____

one ( ) _____ E-mail _____

me _____

dress _____

_____

one ( ) _____ E-mail _____

X

Name

Address

Phone ( ) E-mail

Name

Address

Phone ( ) E-mail

Name

Address

Phone ( ) E-mail

y

Name

Address

Phone ( ) E-mail

Name

Address

Phone ( ) E-mail

ame _____

ddress _____

one ( ) _____ E-mail _____

ame _____

ddress _____

one ( ) _____ E-mail _____

ame _____

ddress _____

one ( ) _____ E-mail _____

me _____

dress _____

one ( ) _____ E-mail _____

me _____

dress _____

one ( ) _____ E-mail _____

z

Name _____

Address _____

_____

Phone (___) _____ E-mail _____

Name _____

Address _____

_____

Phone (___) _____ E-mail _____

Name _____

Address _____

_____

Phone (___) _____ E-mail _____

Name _____

Address _____

_____

Phone (___) _____ E-mail _____

Name _____

Address _____

_____

Phone (___) _____ E-mail _____

ame _____

dress _____

one (_____) _____ E-mail _____

me _____

dress _____

one (_____) _____ E-mail _____

me _____

dress _____

z

one (_____) _____ E-mail _____

me _____

dress _____

ne (_____) _____ E-mail _____

me _____

dress _____

ne (_____) _____ E-mail _____

z

Name

Address

Phone ( )   E-mail

Name

Address

Phone ( )   E-mail

Name

Address

Phone ( )   E-mail

Name

Address

Phone ( )   E-mail

Name

Address

Phone ( )   E-mail